THE THEORY AND PRACTICE OF PEER MENTORING IN SCHOOLS:
How to Recruit, Select, Train and Supervise Peer Mentoring Programs in Educational Settings

BY

REY A. CARR, PH.D.
PEER RESOURCES
http://www.peer.ca

ISBN 978-1-895890-50-1

Publisher:
Peer Resources
1052 Davie Street
Victoria, British Columbia V8S 4E3
Canada
Tel: 1.250.595.3503
Email: info@peer.ca
Web: www.peer.ca
Twitter: www.twitter.com/Peer_Resources

DEDICATION

This work is dedicated to David deRosenroll and Greg Saunders who started out as graduate students and became the full embodiment of mutual peer mentoring, and to the late Stu Conger, whose encouragement to discuss and publish these ideas and practices led to the most fulfilling career possible.

This book is also dedicated to the hundreds of students who graciously allowed themselves to be quizzed, questioned, and photographed to gain information about how peer mentor programs could help them grow, develop and prosper.

Abstract

The overemphasis on the negative aspects of peer pressure has resulted in youth being ignored as a source of positive help to other youth. This article explains the rationale, origins, and practice of peer helping, a system that uses the positive peer pressure skills of empathy and decision-making tools to help others. Young people can be easily trained to use these skills and help others make effective, responsible decisions spanning nearly all aspects of their development.

BONUS Materials Available

Since this white paper was originally written, we have compiled an extensive list of a variety of peer mentor programs and we have tracked all the research associated with this powerful idea. As a reader of this work, you have access to the complete list of peer mentor programs (along with contact information) as well as access to the latest research studies. This information is available to you on our website at http://www.peer.ca

---

For most school counsellors, students are primarily clients who require services in academic, personal-social and career areas. Students are usually seen individually or in groups and are passive recipients of counselling services. Until recently students have been ignored as a resource able to provide assistance to fellow students. In fact, peer culture itself is often seen as a powerful negative force in need of adult control and management. However, without the active help of students in resolving their own psychological problems and crises of human development, it is unlikely that counselling programs or services will be successful or effective. Instead counsellors must engage students as cooperative allies and abandon attempts to win students over through reason or logic. In addition, counsellors must accept the influence power of the existing social network and learn how to enhance the foundations and purposes of the network. Counsellors must also recognize the skills, needs, and behaviours that already are part of a student's repertoire and build on these. Counselling services, then, cannot continue to mold, shape, or force students to fit a model of professional delivery that is alien to the culture it is attempting to serve. Instead, the counselling service must be based on a thorough understanding and use of the factors influencing student development.

Programs or approaches using these development ideas are beginning to emerge and gain credibility. Peer tutoring (Allen, 1976), positive peer culture (Vorrath and Brendtro, 1974) and peer assistance (Carr, 1980; Myrick and Erney, 1978; Varenhorst, 1974), are examples of interventions that draw on principles of development and the values of the existing student network. Peer assistance can be used at many age levels to attend to a variety of problems such as drug and alcohol abuse (Samuels and Samuels, 1975), stress management (Walley, 1980), teenage pregnancies (Foster and Miller, 1980), loneliness (Carr and Saunders, 1979), friendship (Varenhorst, 1978), and widowhood (Romaniuk, Priddy and Romaniuk, 1981). Since it can easily be extended to a variety of other areas such as vocational and career development, the purpose of this article is to describe the origins of peer assistance, illustrate the training model of peer assistance as developed by the Peer assistance Project at the University of Victoria, and relate examples of how peer assistance is practiced in school settings.

What is peer assistance?

Basically peer assistance is a way for students to learn how to care about others and put their caring into practice. It relies strongly on communication skills to facilitate self-exploration and decision-making. Peer assistants are not professional counsellors or therapists. They are students who provide supervised assistance to other students to help think through and reflect on concerns they might be experiencing. A trained peer assistant who is recruited from a core social network can have numerous informal and spontaneous contacts, thus multiplying their impact on a variety of other students. These contacts can enhance the climate of the school and can act as a bridge between professional counselling and students who will not see school counsellors.

Peer assistance is a deliberate and systematic form of psychological education. It enables students to have the skills to implement their powerfully experienced valuing of autonomy and control. By focusing on the process of thinking, feeling, and deciding, rather than evaluating specifically the content, it contributes to the most powerfully experienced need of adolescents: respect. The peer assistant is trained to provide a nonjudgmental listening posture that encourages others to express and explore their concerns, worries, or frustrations. This exploration often prevents self-destructive or other acting-out behaviours by encouraging a student to talk with someone who listens, or "has been there", or can empathize.

Some persons have expressed concern about the word "mentor" being applied to teenagers, and are worried that the term has professional or business connotations. Various programs have accommodated this idea by calling their trained students by other titles such as peer facilitators, peer educators, student support workers or buddies. The importance is not in the title but in how the students relate to other students, and the way in which these relationships can be used to enhance their development. We typically use the term "peer assistance" as an umbrella term to cover the wide range of positive helping relationships students can have with other students.

What are the origins of peer assistance?

In order to understand the training and program operations of peer assistance it may be useful to briefly explore the nine foundation areas which have significantly contributed to its creation and led to its natural development.

Over the past few years, a number of large-scale evaluations of school counselling have taken place across Canada (Carr, 1978; Guerette, 1981; Haughey and Bowman, 1980). While these studies had somewhat different purposes, were conducted with a variety of student populations and used different survey instruments, some of their conclusions are remarkably similar: only a minority of students ever go to see counsellors. Most students, when experiencing some kind of personal concern, rely primarily on their friends as sources of help. With only minor changes in percentages these findings hold true regardless of age level, quality of counselling available, or experience in working with a counsellor. Similar studies conducted in the United States (Prediger, Roth and Noeth, 1974) have demonstrated the same results; namely, that friends remain the number one in-school resource for students considering personal decisions, job plans, and how far to go with formal education.

A second foundation for peer assistance comes from research on the helping relationship itself (Carkhuff, 1969; Egan, 1975; and Ivey, 1971). The skills associated with effective helping have not only been described and demystified, but have also been shown to be learnable by a variety of lay persons, including paraprofessionals (Carkhuff, 1969), high school students (Carr and Saunders, 1979), junior high students (Carr, McDowell and McKee, 1981), and elementary age students (Bowman and Myrick, 1980). The training itself can also serve as a form of treatment and the peer assistants enhance their own development and psychological growth. An important implication of helping skill research is that the skills are not only helpful, but can be taught to younger persons so that they can be used within the youth culture. While a number of recent therapy advances appear promising (neurolinguistic programming, for example), it remains unclear as to whether young people can learn to use these approaches.

Across North America, high school students have responded to surveys designed to assess what they see as the major problems confronting youth today (Carr, 1980). The results, which serve as the third foundation block, consistently reveal that loneliness or making and keeping friends are either the highest or among the top five concerns of young people. These self-reported rankings often differ remarkably from adult rankings of what adults perceive as the major problems concerning youth. This difference is an example of a potential "generation gap" which may prevent students from seeking help from adults.

More seriously, even though friendship concerns occupy a major proportion of students' time, and as Rubin (1980) has stated, are often the sources of greatest pleasure and deepest frustration, social scientists have paid virtually no attention to them. It is likely that friends can help each other learn things that are unique and cannot be taught by parents or educators. Debilitating conditions at home can often be neutralized through involvement with peers in school (Rubin, 1980). Contrary to popular opinion, friendship patterns do not remain stable within the school context, and it appears that the purposes of friendship change as students get older. Senior high students describe a friend as a person who listens, helps, and communicates in depth. Friendships are characterized by <u>mutuality</u> or a willingness to be helpers to each other.

Many teenagers have already learned how to make friends and they remain quite popular with their peers, even though sometimes not liked by their teachers. These students have acquired certain skills such as abilities to be attentive and supportive, to manage conflicts appropriately, to be sensitive to others and express thoughts and ideas in way that others do no feel their esteem is threatened. And while knowledge of how to make and keep friends can contribute to success, it is only secondary to an ability and willingness to use the skills in a practical way. Students who possess these skills are more often than not unaware of what they actually do on a conscious basis. These students when involved in reflective-oriented training can learn very easily how to teach others to do what they do to make and keep friends.

The fourth basis for using students to help other students comes from the emphasis on primary prevention (Albee and Joffe, 1981) within the mental health movement and with the application of preventive counselling (Carr, 1976) within school settings. Prevention programs have a two level thrust: the need to strengthen (or immunize) students against harmful influences (by providing skills in resolving problems more effectively) and at the same time reduce the incidence of psychologically destructive factors within the environment (eliminate an uncaring environment, for example).

Student needs for competency (to be strong), intelligence (not academic, but to know the scene, keep from getting conned), responsible role taking (to be respected) and self-esteem (to be valued and understood) form the basis for foundation five. Students recognize how powerful these needs are and often direct their best-shot, put down comments in these directions: "baby, boring, suck, dumb, stupid, weird, retard"; and their best compliments as: "fox, Mr. Macho, cool, got-it-together". Adults often react to the superficial manifestations of these needs with patronizing, scornful, or disrespectful behaviour (often with the intention of "helping"), but the students, being intensely sensitive to the needs, will retreat further, fight back, or become self-destructive. They generally turn to other students who have shared similar embarrassing, humiliating, or need-ignoring experiences and who will listen, not to approve or disapprove, but to accept and understand. Research and knowledge about human development closely parallels student needs and serves as the sixth foundation. A key issue in adolescence is independence, but as Ivey (1977) has pointed out, it is important to understand independence in relation to peer culture perspectives. For example, Coleman (1980) has discovered that, for teenage boys, independence means freedom from constraint, the freedom in life to become what one wishes; whereas, for girls, independence means internal freedom, or the opportunity to be one's self and to have some autonomy with respect to one's feelings and thoughts.

Adolescence has also been described as a time of identity seeking, using Erikson's terms, securing identify and avoiding identity diffusion. Yet all too often counsellors have assumed this time to be a teenager's search for the "real self", when, in fact, it is less of a time when one finds oneself and more of a time when one makes oneself. It is the daily interactions and experience (or lack of) with fellow students that shape the self-perception more dramatically than any amount of self-reflection or intelligence.

Despite the glut of textbooks on adolescent development, very little is really known about individual differences among teenagers. For example, as a development specialist, it is clear to me that the power of the peer group is not only greatly misunderstood but also grossly exaggerated. This is perpetuated by adults seeing all teenagers as the same and ignoring the developmental process which experiences important changes and differences in friendship, group memberships, motivation and values. Counsellors may be particularly insensitive to the social evolution of the peer group or cliques and tend to overrate their impact and influences as well as misunderstand their constructive role.

The effects of peers tutoring peers (Allen, 1976; Gartner, Kohler and Reissman, 1971) has received considerable attention and serves as another foundation block. Generally, the research on tutoring supports the value of using peers to improve the achievement and esteem of other students. Research has suggested that tutoring is as helpful for the tutor as for the tutee (Chandler, 1980) and that student-tutors may surpass teacher-tutors in tutoring some students (Karegianes, Pascarella and Pflaum, 1980). In addition many students prefer to learn from peers, and evidence gathered by Price (1980) on student learning styles, indicates that students are less teacher- motivated in the higher grades and that low motivated, learning disabled students are more likely to be peer-oriented. Research by Shaefer (1980) and Condry and Siman (1976) has revealed that peer-oriented students become dependent on the peer group not by choice but by necessity because of a lack of attention and affection at home. This shift occurs around sixth grade, and is followed by pre-delinquent behaviour in grades seven and eight.

The increasing popularity of self-help (Romeder, 1981) or mutual aid groups (Peavy, 1978) provides the eighth origin for peer assistance. Basically, these groups are formed by peers whose mutual needs are often unmet by. existing services or who are unable or unwilling to use available institutions. They meet to address shared or common concerns and often rely on the relationship of member to member to resolve problems, using support and catharsis as a problem-solving intervention. Probably the most famous and most successful (in terms of longevity, participation, and outcomes) is Alcoholics Anonymous. Women's groups, Weight Watchers, cancer patients, family groups, single parents, Parents of Murdered Children are just a few additional examples. Adolescents have formed their own mutual aid groups, yet the positive, coping functions of these groups to assist in the healthy development of teenagers have virtually been ignored for the more sensationalist negative or conflict producing behaviours. While we have no formal research to support our observations, it appears that kids aged 8 to 12 also tend to form groups or mouse packs, thus indicating an earlier age for peer orientation.

Finally, the last foundation for peer assistance is based on the costs and availability of professionals. The historic 1961 report of the Joint Commission on Mental Illness clearly specified the need to improve community resources rather than to spend extensive funds on professional training. Despite increases in professional personnel and advances in effective therapeutic interventions, the problems of teenagers continue to outpace the growth and availability of formal help. Skyrocketing costs for services, unmanageable case loads and long waiting lists, growing cynicism about the skills of professionals, and frightening statistics about adolescent death and disability, violence and depression require the enlistment of adolescents themselves in helping each other. Students generally know much sooner than adults when another student is experiencing trouble and can be in close, more spontaneous contact. Peer assistants supplement existing counselling services and can free counsellors to work with or refer seriously troubled students. Peer assistants can also serve as a bridge to get a troubled friend involved in professional help.

The Peer Assistance Model

Having examined the foundations of peer assistance, we can now turn to how programs are organized, what is involved in training, and how students work with other students.

As with any successful intervention it is important to develop a strong practical foundation upon which the program can rely. We begin by assessing the needs of the client population (using surveys, interviews, observations, etc.) to determine whether peer assistance is the most appropriate or highest priority intervention for improving student psychological health. We also enlist the support of parent groups, teaching staff, etc., by forming advisory committees or having them involved in the training. While counsellors appear to be the most likely persons to run or organize peer assistance, they are often unavailable or highly reluctant. Involving non-counsellor personnel is often beneficial because it encourages and supports the helping interests of other persons within the school context. Parents are often the most enthusiastic group, and have quickly seen the value of improving the quality of student to student help.

We also insure the objectives for the program are clear and written out. In addition, we assess the training skills of the trainers and provide training courses for persons interested in training students. Initially, the Peer assistance Project personnel began by training the students ourselves, primarily to insure that our training approach was appropriate for adolescents. Having satisfied ourselves that training was appropriate and having trained a variety of different groups, we realized it would be more efficient and empowering for us to train others to do the training and then remain available to consult with them on problems they encountered.

The final element of the start-up process concerns thinking through trainee selection procedures, preparing a systematic model of training, and creating an approach to evaluation. The next steps after building the foundation are recruiting and selecting students, delivering the training itself to small groups, providing supervised assignments, and supervising the program itself. Since these areas have a strong practical base, and because we have been asked a number of times to respond to questions in these areas, each of them will be detailed here.

Recruiting and Selection

Since peer assistance is based on the well-documented evidence that peers seek help from peers, it is clear that many students are already providing some kind of help to other students. For training purposes it is helpful if these students can identify themselves through requests for volunteers who are interested in counselling or helping. We generally ask two questions to help volunteers become interested: "have you ever tried to help a friend, but didn't know what to do?" and "do you know what it's like to have worries, concerns, frustrations?" In addition to seeking volunteers, we encourage students to nominate other students and staff to nominate students (sometimes these nominations are quite different from each other). We also ask parents, and from our observations of students in the school, we nominate potential students. Finally, we encourage the use of empirical nominations that can serve as both identifying and verifying activities. Examples of such approaches include sociograms (who talks to whom), class play techniques ("who would you choose to play the role of a people helper in this play?"). We also identify using student vernacular, such as what are the identifiable social groups in the school (for examples, "heads, greasers, sucks"), and ask if they know people who fit in more than one group. Actually, we draw circles on a blackboard representing each of the groups students identify, and we show the circles intersecting, so that at one point all the circles overlap (part of our definition of a network), and ask the students who they know that would fit into the intersections. We then will make written and personal requests of the student names received from a variety of nominations and, together with the volunteers, hold an information meeting. The meeting is advertised through bulletins, announcements, word-of-mouth, posters, lunches, staff meetings, speakers programs, and in-class recruiting. Once a program has been initiated, peer assistants can take over these activities in order to implement the philosophy of students speaking to students. Vocational education programs have begun to realize that teen-to-teen communication may be the most effective method to reach teenage audiences (Walton and Howard, 1980).

Many programs that have implemented our approach find a high number of female students volunteering. This is easy to understand since these young women are often more aware of their values of caring and expressing concern for others. We modify this imbalance by encouraging them to directly recruit or talk to male students. This has had dramatic effects in bringing in the young men.

At the information meeting we describe the training, its potential uses, and ask who would be interested. From questions they ask, we can infer student interests ("Can I take this in place of geometry? Will it be after school? Will there be course credit?"). At this meeting we usually ask a question of our own to make sure a peer assistance program fits in with student needs: "Would such a program be of value in your school?" The answer is always a resounding "yes". Generally, there are more volunteers than can be trained at any one time, so we work out a schedule that puts students on a waiting list. For research-oriented persons this waiting list can serve as a control group (we have done this). If parent permission is necessary, and we think it should be—partly to inform and educate parents through the permission letter itself, and in part to insure their support—permission forms are distributed to the students at the information meeting. We make sure the letter has enough detail in it so that parents can make informed decisions. Anybody who works with students and sends things home to get signed knows how frustrating it can be trying to get them back; however, we have found the letters return quickly, sometimes with handwritten post scripts praising the idea. Students also have commented on discussions they have with their parents about the program that have been stimulating and encouraging.

When the letter comes back we hold interviews with each student during which time we ask them about themselves, their experiences in relating to others and we try to assess their learning style. This can be done with a specific instrument such as the Inventory developed by Dunn and Dunn, (1978). We give them feedback about their style and we are primarily looking to see how interested they are in hearing about themselves. A decision to advance to training is made solely on the basis of two behavioural criteria: a) are they receptive to knowing about themselves, and b) do they have <u>severe</u> emotional problems which would make them unable to use the training or interfere with the training. If the answer is yes to this second question, we will discuss possible referral with them to either school or community resources. We have underlined severe above because we often make a clinical judgment here, since students experiencing a variety of developmental problems can not only benefit from the training, but serve as excellent helpers for students with similar concerns. However, since the major goal of peer assistant training is to <u>increase</u> the number of students who

have and <u>use</u> helping skills, the training should not be used as a
substitute for group counselling or guidance courses.

Training Process

We divide students into separate training groups of six to eight, and
the training consists of two phases. The first phase consists of 12 to
16 training sessions, one to two hours in duration, which we ideally
like to schedule twice a week, so that initial training takes about six
to eight weeks. The second phase consists of a series of supervised
assignments resembling a practicum, and weekly supervision
meetings are held with students in groups of 10 to 12. Since we are
strongly committed to a learning-based model of training, we have
structured each training session with a systematic process to
maximize student skill development. Each session begins with
<u>continuity</u>, where old business is discussed, concerns are
expressed, opportunities for caring and sharing with others given,
and homework is discussed. We then move to the <u>awareness</u> portion
where a description or directions are given for today's session; the
rationale and purpose are briefly stated; students make a self-
calibration and/or declare their need concerning the topic and
relate how it might fit them from their frame of reference. We next
emphasize <u>know-how</u>, where we provide a demonstration, deliver a
lecturette, and use group techniques such as creative use of
brainstorming, role play or modelling. Following this is the
<u>assertiveness</u> section where students work in pairs, or trios doing
simulation or other experiential activities. We then move to the
<u>process</u> phase where observers give feedback; we inquire as to the

quality of experience; and work towards synthesis, integration, and summarizing. The session concludes with a <u>practice</u> phase where homework is assigned and then we start the cycle again with <u>continuity</u> at the next session. Homework is often an applied assignment focused on generalizing the learning from the session to the cultural world of the student. We closely monitor these steps and discover at many times a particular spot where we cannot move on to the next step because we haven't adequately covered a previous step. We rely continuously on feedback, observation and actual skill performance, and may recycle back to a particular step.

Training Content

We have identified twelve core topics that are essential to peer assistance and we have detailed the step-by-step procedures for the activities in our training manuals, *The Peer Helping Starter Kit* (Carr & Saunders, 1979); *Out of the Mainstream Youth Peer Program Training Materials and Resources* (Carr & DeRosenroll, 1995); and *The Mentor Program Development Resources Kit* (Carr, DeRosenroll, & Saunders, 1991). The content we cover consists of: getting acquainted with strangers; attending skills; roadblocks to better communication; self-disclosure and expression of feelings; listening; empathy training; questioning; assertiveness or "I messages"; feedback skills; values clarification; decision-making; problem-solving; ethics; confidentiality; and referral. (These manuals are available at http://www.peer.ca/pubs.html)

Once the core skills have been reasonably mastered we recommend that programs develop practicum topics from the experiences of the students trying to implement their new skills. We recognize they may feel awkward, mechanical or phony, so we accept this as part of the learning process and help them locate their feelings or thoughts. Handling silence; talking to students whose behaviours you don't dig; trying the skills in a group setting; and getting rebuffed are all examples of specific problems students bring up which we turn into training sessions.

The final elements of the training takes place during supervision when special topics are introduced which relate to specific problems such as drugs, parents, career decisions, pregnancy. We may introduce speakers (who support process learning) to talk about certain areas or we may do refreshers in the core area.

Our training model begins with a pre-determined structure and ends with a student-determined structure. We retain the emphasis on process throughout, yet we are sensitive to the needs of the students so that neither the structure nor the process act as a barrier to truly understanding and fully relating to our student trainees. In other words, we remain student-centered rather than strictly agenda-centered.

Assignments as Peer Assistants

When the approximately thirty hours of training has been completed, the trainer(s) meet(s) with each student individually, and applying the guidelines from the activities on feedback, discuss with the student how they did on the training, what age level or kinds of problems they would like to deal with, the type of setting or context, and the readiness of the student to take the training again, and they are given assistant status. We have certificates that look like diplomas that we give to the students as a way of giving formal recognition. We have developed five major categories of assignments: group activities, outreach/alert, one-on-one, elementary focus, and external programs.

Group activities include team sports, clubs or other formal groups which exist in the school and in which the student is already a participant. The assignment is to look for ways to use the skills in these groups (a fellow team member is looking discouraged after having struck out for the fourth time; a member loses a chess match; or just normal conversations about concerns of youth). Students may also get involved in informal or "rap" groups, or participate in special groups structured to deal with certain problems such as divorce, loss, drugs, pregnancy, and other areas of concern.

The outreach/alert assignments support the student in tuning into their existing network, or paying attention to clues which may indicate another student is having difficulty (a student slams a locker, a student is crying in the washroom, a student sits alone and dejected on the playing field, etc.). These informal and spontaneous contacts are the core of peer assistance. The peer assistants usually experience immediate acceptance from the troubled student, once that person sees that the peer offers genuine listening and caring. Since this helping is dependent on the students becoming involved in the many social networks in the school, we anticipated during our early training experiences that the peer assistants would become an elite clique of their own. Yet this has not happened. Though they remain friendly towards each other, they do not socialize together, and retain themselves in their primary social networks. In a sense, this reaffirms the need for and success of a broad selection process.

One-on-one assignments are usually based on a referral process, where potential "clients" may be referred to the trainer (coordinator) by parents, counsellors, or teachers. The coordinator reviews the referral with the adult to determine its appropriateness and specificity. An assigned peer assistant then talks to the referring adult, and the adult introduces the student to the peer assistant. We encourage the peer assistant to have their first meeting with the student over lunch because food is friendly, there is a specific time limit, and if it doesn't work out, they can always eat. Once the student and the peer assistant begin meeting, progress is reviewed, and modifications are made if the peer assistant is in over their head.

Sometimes these referrals are just attempts to help students get to know older students and feel less lost or alone or enhance their self-esteem ("wow, a twelfth grader is spending time with me!"). Other referrals can be for specific problems, including academic difficulties, and a peer assistant may engage in tutoring. We have found our tutors to be keenly aware of the feelings a low achieving student expresses about being able to do certain academic work, and the peer assistant/tutor often can give encouragement, support, and teaching in a more effective way than a tutor who doesn't pay attention to the feelings of inadequacy of the tutee.

Some peer assistants want to work with elementary age children, so arrangements are made with neighbouring schools to use these students to lead groups, talk with individuals, help with orientations, or work on the playground. Other students may become associated with another external program such as a recreation centre or peer assistant training in another school or community context. We have plans to use many of the trained peer assistants as summer street workers, aiding the groups of kids who gather at various locations on a regular basis throughout the city during the lengthy summer vacations.

Regardless of assignment, formal or informal, on or off-campus, the students meet weekly in a group to discuss their progress with their supervisor. While the names of "clients" are not discussed, the kinds of concerns brought up or discussed are, with an emphasis on the peer assistants' perception of how they handled the situations and the skills they used. Sometimes it is clear that certain skills may need refreshing, so a workshop is scheduled; other times it is clear that there is a commonality to the problems "clients" are bringing up, and that a possible system-oriented intervention can be developed and presented to change makers. These weekly meetings enable the peer assistants to experience

1. How many of you have been thinking about your own career during the last month? That is, how many have had thoughts or concerns about your career choice or progress or are thinking about changing jobs, retiring, advancing, etc.?
2. Formulate these thoughts, feelings into a statement such as, "During the last month, I've been seriously considering ...". (Write it down, briefly.)
3. Now think about how the person next to you might be able to help you with this consideration. What would be, in your view, the most important thing they could do to help you with what you've been thinking about?

support and autonomy while at the same time they see that they are not alone in trying to help other students work towards effective solutions to frustrating problems.

In summary, we support efforts of counsellors to discover additional ways to involve students as resources in the counselling process. As long as students are forced to play passive roles, areas like career guidance will suffer. The counsellor as expert may encourage student passivity. Even advances in computer technology may only give students the illusion of control. We also support a systems-oriented approach that works to understand and accept negative or problematic elements of culture as challenges to be used rather than eliminated. Thirdly, we support a strong focus on developmental psychology in order to recognize superficial expressions of concern, and rather than discard them, use these concerns as avenues for deeper exploration. Adolescents are facile at "smokescreens" to cover up fears and anxieties. Their search for meaning during the early years may look like conflicts over lipstick and tight clothing, but it is symbolic of concern for self. Their concerns about dating in middle adolescence may look like sexual activity, but it is a search for interpersonal competence. Finally, in later adolescence, conflicts with adults over values and ideas are strong attempts to find meaning in their lives.

We conclude with an exercise we often use for helping adults identify their own peer-related decision-making in order to test out the power of friendship relations throughout the life cycle.

References

Action for mental health: Final report of the Joint Commission on Mental Illness and Health (1961). New York: Basic Books.

Albee, G, & Joffe, J., (Eds) (1981). *The issues: An overview of primary prevention.* Hanover, New Hampshire: University Press of New England.

Allen, V. L. (Ed.) (1976). *Children as teachers: Theory and research on tutoring.* New York: Academic Press.

Bowman, R., & Myrick, R. (1980). "I'm a junior counselor, having lots of fun." *The School Counselor. 28,* 1, 31-39.

Carkhuff, R. (1969). *Helping and human relations: A primer for lay and professional helpers.* New York: Holt, Rinehart and Winston.

Carr, R. (1976). The effects of preventive counselling with elementary school principals to change teacher staff meeting behaviours. *Canadian Counsellor, 10,* 4, 156-166.

Carr, R. (1978). *The state of school counselling in British Columbia.* Vancouver, BC: Education Research Institute of British Columbia.

Carr, R., & DeRosenroll, D. (1995). *Out of the mainstream youth peer program training and resource kit.* Victoria, BC: Peer Systems Consulting Group, Inc.

Carr, R., DeRosenroll, & Saunders, G. (1991). *The mentor program development resource kit.* Victoria, BC: Peer Systems Consulting Group, Inc..

Carr, R., & Saunders, G. (1979). *The peer assistant starter kit.* Victoria, B.C. Peer Assistance Project, University of Victoria.

Carr, R. (1980). Students helping students. *Reed Career Magazine, 2,* 4, 24-26.

Carr, R. (1980). *[Adolescent and adult ranking of problems confronting adolescents],* Unpublished raw data.

Carr, R., McDowell, & McKee, M. (1981, May). *Peer assistance at the junior secondary level.* Paper presented at the Canadian Guidance and Counselling Association Conference, Calgary, Alberta.

Chandler, T. (1980).Reversal peer tutoring effects on powerlessness in adolescents. *Adolescence, 15,* 59, 715-722.

Coleman, J. (1980). *Relationships in adolescence.* London: Cambridge University Press

Condry, J., & Siman, M. (1976). Characteristics of peer- and adult-oriented children. *Journal of Marriage and the Family, 36,* 3, 543-554.

Dunn, R., & Dunn, K. (1978). *Teaching students through their individual learning styles.* Reston, Virginia: Reston Publishing Company, Inc.

Egan, G. (1975). *The skilled helper: A model for systematic helping and interpersonal relating.* Monterey, California: Brooks/Cole.

Gartner, A., Kohler, M. & Reissman, F. (1971). *Children teach children.* New York: Harper and Row.

Guerette, J.L. (1981, January). *Needs for more personal counselling in schools.* Paper presented at the Seventh National Consultation on Vocational Counselling. Ottawa.

Haughey, J. & Bowman, J. (1980). *Counselling and guidance services in selected junior high schools: Utilization and identified need.* Winnipeg: Department of Education, Research Branch.

Ivey, A. (1971). *Microcounselling.* Springfield, Il: Thomas.

Ivey, A. (1977). Cultural expertise: Toward systematic outcome criteria in counselling and psychoeducation. *Personnel and Guidance Journal, 55,* 296-302.

Karegianes, M., Pascarella, E., Pflaum, S. (1980). The effects of peer editing on the writing proficiency of low-achieving tenth grade students. *Journal of Educational Research, 36,* 5, 203-206.

Myrick, R., & Erney, T. (1978). *Youth helping youth: A handbook for training peer facilitators.* Minneapolis: Educational Media Corporation.

Peavy, V. (1978). *Adults helping adults: An existential approach to cooperative counselling.* Victoria, BC: University of Victoria, Adult Counselling Project.

Prediger, D., Roth, J., & Noeth, R. (1974). Career development of youth: A nationwide study. *Personnel and Guidance Journal, 53,* 97-104.

Price, G. (1980, July). *Research using the learning style inventory.* Paper presented at Second annual conference on teaching students through their individual learning styles. New York City.

Romaniuk, M., Priddy, J., & Romaniuk, J. (1981). Older peer assistant training. *Counsellor Education and Supervision, 20,* 3, 225-232.

Romeder, J.M. (1981). Self-help groups and mental health: A promising avenue. *Canada's Mental Health, 29,* 1, 10-314.

Rubin, Z. (1980). *Children's friendships.* Cambridge, MA: Harvard University Press.

Samuels, D., & Samuels, M. (1975). *The complete handbook of peer counseling.* Miami: Fiesta Publishing Corporation.

Shaefer, C. (1980). The impact of the peer culture in the residential treatment of youth. *Adolescence, 15,* 60, 831-845.

Varenhorst, B. (1974). Training adolescents as peer assistants. *Personnel and Guidance Journal, 53,* 4, 271-275.

Varenhorst, B. (1978). *Curriculum guide for student peer counseling training.* Palo Alto, California: Palo Alto Unified School District.

Vorrath, H., & Brendtro, L. (1974). *Positive peer culture.* New York: Aldine Publishing Company.

Walley, W. (1980, September). *CTU begins educators support program.* Chicago Union Teacher.

Walton, L., & Howard, P. (1980). The student connection. *VocEd., 55,* 9, 40-43.

PROGRAM OVERVIEW

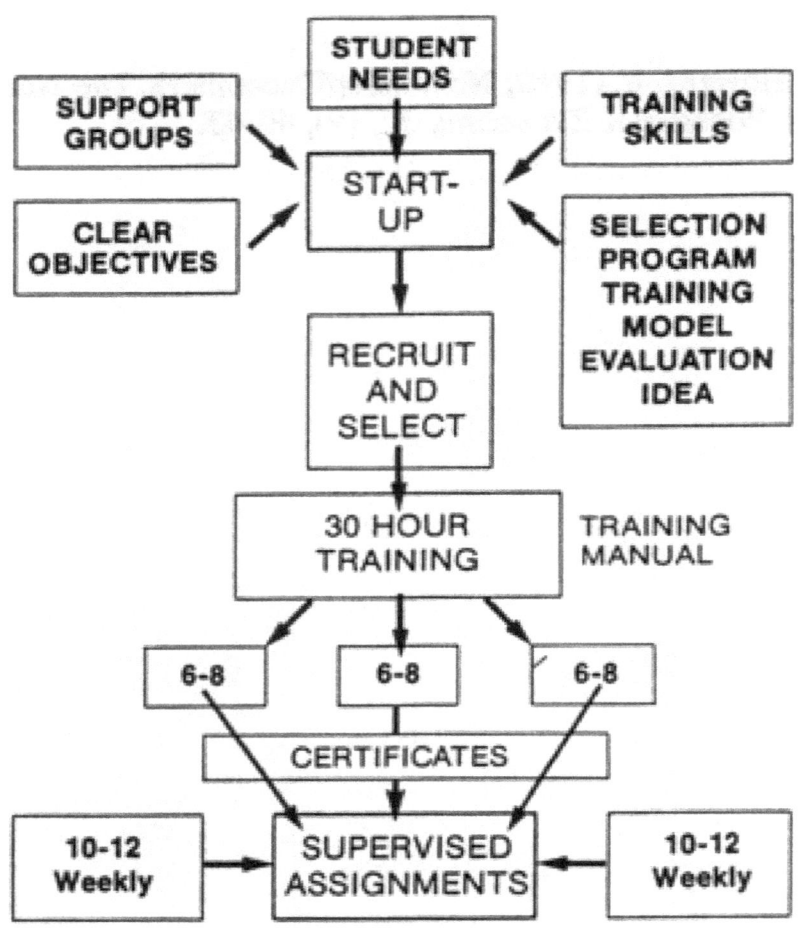

SELECTION PROCESS

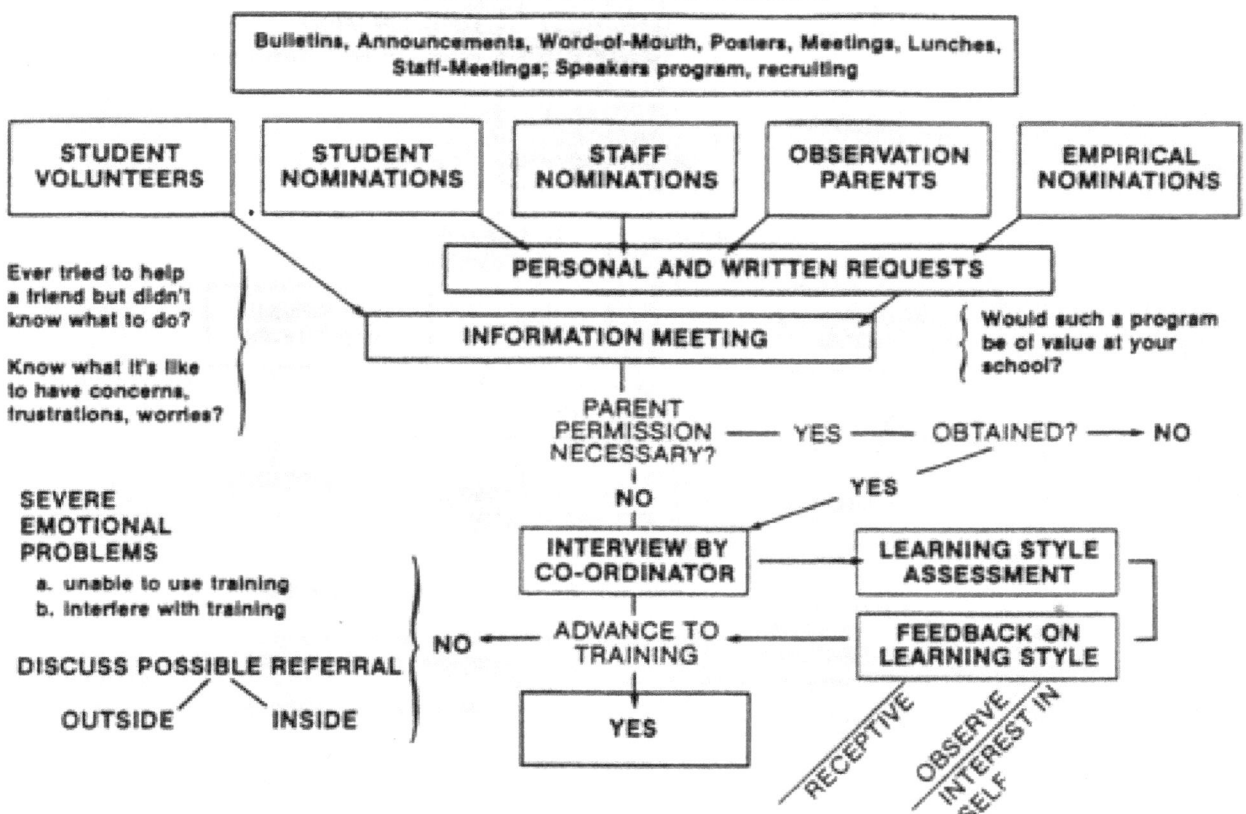

Bulletins, Announcements, Word-of-Mouth, Posters, Meetings, Lunches, Staff-Meetings; Speakers program, recruiting

| STUDENT VOLUNTEERS | STUDENT NOMINATIONS | STAFF NOMINATIONS | OBSERVATION PARENTS | EMPIRICAL NOMINATIONS |

PERSONAL AND WRITTEN REQUESTS

Ever tried to help a friend but didn't know what to do?

Know what it's like to have concerns, frustrations, worries?

INFORMATION MEETING

Would such a program be of value at your school?

PARENT PERMISSION NECESSARY? —— YES —— OBTAINED? —▸ NO

NO   YES

SEVERE EMOTIONAL PROBLEMS
a. unable to use training
b. interfere with training

INTERVIEW BY CO-ORDINATOR ——▸ LEARNING STYLE ASSESSMENT

DISCUSS POSSIBLE REFERRAL

NO ◀—— ADVANCE TO TRAINING ◀—— FEEDBACK ON LEARNING STYLE

OUTSIDE   INSIDE

YES

RECEPTIVE   OBSERVE INTEREST IN SELF

ASSIGNMENT MAP

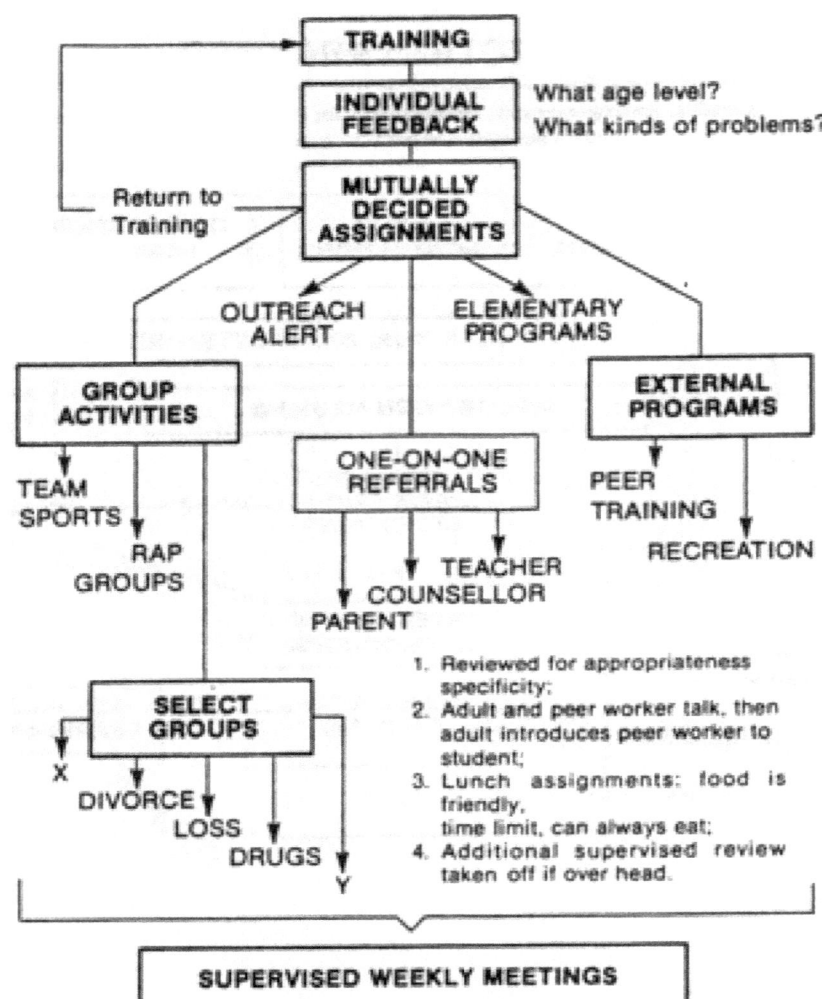

TRAINING

INDIVIDUAL FEEDBACK

What age level?
What kinds of problems?

Return to Training

MUTUALLY DECIDED ASSIGNMENTS

OUTREACH ALERT

ELEMENTARY PROGRAMS

GROUP ACTIVITIES

EXTERNAL PROGRAMS

ONE-ON-ONE REFERRALS

TEAM SPORTS

RAP GROUPS

PEER TRAINING

RECREATION

PARENT

COUNSELLOR

TEACHER

SELECT GROUPS

X

DIVORCE

LOSS

DRUGS

Y

1. Reviewed for appropriateness specificity;
2. Adult and peer worker talk, then adult introduces peer worker to student;
3. Lunch assignments: food is friendly, time limit, can always eat;
4. Additional supervised review taken off if over head.

SUPERVISED WEEKLY MEETINGS

TRAINING PROCESS

CONTINUITY — Old business, concerns, sharing & caring, homework discussion

AWARENESS — Description/direction; rationale/purpose, self calibration, declaration o need, ability, personal frame of reference.

KNOW-HOW —
Presentation, lecturette, group techniques: creative use, brainstorming, role play, model

ASSERTIVENESS —
In-class pairs, trios, simulations, experiential activities

PROCESS — Observer feedback, experience inquiry, synthesis, integration, summarization (learning style)

PRACTICE — Homework assignments

CONTINUITY

ORIGINS OF PEER SUPPORT WORK

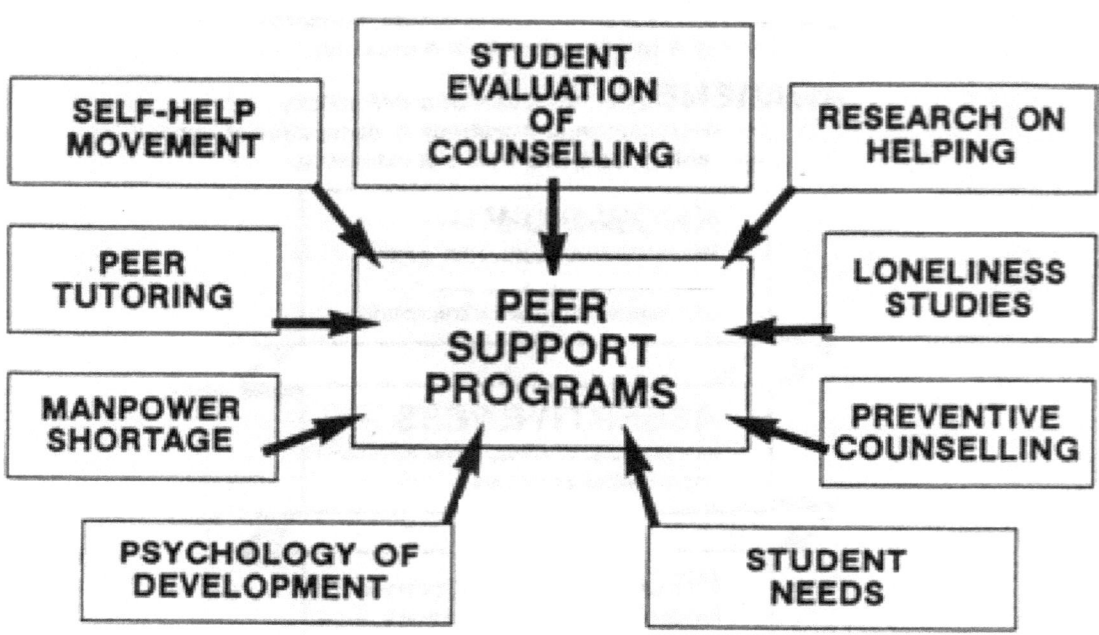

CPSIA information can be obtained
at www.ICGtesting.com
Printed in the USA
LVHW061537070720
659997LV00008B/559